THE WIRE-THIN BRIDE

THE WIRE-THIN BRIDE

Cornelia Hoogland

TURNSTONE PRESS

Turnstone Press
607-100 Arthur Street
Winnipeg, Manitoba
Canada   R3B 1H3

Turnstone Press gratefully acknowledges the assistance of the Canada Council and the Manitoba Arts Council.

Cover illustration: Marcia Perkins, pencil on mylar.

This book was printed by Hignell Printing Limited for Turnstone Press.

Printed and bound in Canada.

Canadian Cataloguing in Publication Data

Hoogland, Joan Cornelia, 1952-

The wire-thin bride

Poems.
ISBN 0-88801-147-4

I. Title.

PS8565.O63W5 1990   C811'.54   C90-097033-2
PR9199.3.H66W5 1990

ACKNOWLEDGEMENTS

Some of these poems, or versions of them, first appeared in
Antigonish Review, *arc*, *Arts Scarborough*, *Ariel*, *blue buffalo*,
CBC Alberta Anthology, *CV2*, *Dandelion*, *Edges*, *Event*,
Malahat Review, *Massachusetts Review*, *Poet's Gallery*, *Prairie
Journal of Canadian Literature*, *Prism International*, *Skylines*,
The World and I and *Whetstone*.

"Garage Sale" appeared as "Will You Be Easier To Please
Next Time?" in *Garden Varieties*, an anthology of the League
of Canadian Poets, Cormorant Press, 1988.

The section of poems, "How Our Feet Go On," appeared in
Dutch Voices, Netherlandic Press, 1989.

I would like to thank my Calgary writing community,
Marcia Perkins, Walter Zwirner, and particularly
Christopher Wiseman, for encouraging and helping me in
individual ways as I prepared this book. Thanks to Adele
Wiseman and the faculty at the Banff Centre for the Arts;
also to Don Coles.

To these four:

Walter, Danielle, Cameron and Tenille

CONTENTS

1. THE MERMAID'S BALE

Garage Sale / 3
Hoard / 4
From Towers / 5
Frog Prince / 6
Spider Lake / 7
In the Mountains / 8
Details / 9
Really Alone / 10
White Bread and Cake / 11
The Name You Didn't Want / 13
Gold Against Carnelian / 14
The Man I Love Is Going / 15
Thirst / 16
After Babysitting, Coming Home / 17

2. IN THE GALLERY
(After seeing Marcia Perkins' drawings, *Studies From Life*)

1. Artist / 21
2. Referent / 22
3. In the Gallery / 23
4. Kicking Stones / 24
5. Man Sawn in 1/2 / 25
6. Lesson in the Anatomy Lab / 26
7. What We Are / 27
8. Bust / 28
9. Untitled / 29

3. WHAT I KNOW OF HER

There Are Tides of Sky That Pull / 33
Watching My Mother Dress / 34
Shore-Knitter / 35
Her Full-Cupboard Strength / 36
Graduation Ceremony / 37
First Born / 38
Strand / 39
Coming for Mother / 40
What I Know of Her / 41

4. HOW OUR FEET GO ON / 43

5. STORY, LOVE

Poem at Christmastime / 63
My Son / 64
Letting Betsy Go / 66
Choir Robes / 68
Photograph of a Split-Fern / 69
New World / 70
Unlovely Behind the Door / 71
The Time I Knew You Long Before We Met / 73
A Song That's Over Too Soon / 74
Doubles / 75
The Bridge You Forgot / 76
After Messiah / 77
Love Letters / 78
I'll Never Live Where It Doesn't Snow / 80
Postcard from the Reading Room, British Library / 81
"If You Ever Get to Tbilsk I Will Show You What I Mean" / 82

1. THE MERMAID'S BALE

GARAGE SALE

The air's starched with winter.
Under the shredded banners of trees
a wedding dress swings from a branch.
Wind fills the skirt, hucks it against a black thigh.
Icy lace cleaves to the shoulders of the wire-thin bride.

And photographs—

> *Here's me in my wedding dress.*
> *My bouquet. O how the smell*
> *of those freesias lingered.*
> *We used real flowers then.*

A whole raft of unlikely goods—
china for four, the album, rondo
by Chopin; summer nights
chucked on frozen ground. And that dress
hanging unholy in the trees.
Its long cold look.

HOARD

One pound of butter and Christmas
still months away.
In the dark downstairs light
from the opened freezer yellow
as cream. The foil package a star
among loaves. She'd peel
back a smell rich as almond.

I thought of Nel when you left
bottles of Medoc and Bourgogne
behind the dusky blue pane of the cabinet.
Her Baking Day was any, set aside.
She'd take the butter and cut and blend
cookies into celebrations.
Nothing was empty to her—she'd fill
a bottle with babies breath
and have a vase.

Nel knew it starts with letting go
a butter hoard. I lift the bottle,
pry loose the image that surrounds it.
A star splashes into the broodings
of memory; all I can hold close
is already there, rich
and spilling.

FROM TOWERS
    (for Rachel Wyatt)

On the veranda, that small proud lip
of the mountains, two women
sip berry juice with stir-sticks of licorice.

And one is Rapunzel, and one is the witch
who says she's the mother, and this is the tower.

On the other side of the glass door
sits a bald man, ear looped with gold.
He holds a girl-hand in his big one
and her nails become marble skins
of reptiles. He paints the hidden out.

Her tangled fear of roots.

The elder woman raises her hand that appears
like a small globe of citrus above the mountains.
It's yours, you can . . . and as she speaks
wind lifts and fills the great skirts
the women wear, layer by layer,
till they are open as dinner plates.

The forest is dark.
Reaches its hungry limbs
to the woman small as a child up there.

Her hair grows inches.

                            Banff, Alberta.

FROG PRINCE

The first time you said no.
So I dreamed you
in my room, shirt off for a shower,
I by the window, hands in my lap.
Outside it was spring.
On the white spread your shirt
a pool of blue.

In the kitchen
petals of the Japanese plum
through the window.
Josephine at the sink peels carrots;
strokes the blade against the curling skins.
I feel you, watchful, and your arms
open. I go to you,
           past you
           to the pond
           where I'll seize a coming true
           by its warty legs.

Plain thing, if I hurl you to the wall,
will you, will you?

SPIDER LAKE

I love swimming the deep
water of the inlet's embrace,
dark with shoregreen.

At the smooth centre
her heavy belly hangs
black. We splash upward,
noises fanning into air,
and beach our tired bodies on her
island eye
before swimming long limbs back.

I love her cold, moist
humour, the wash
of her fingers holding me
buoyant until
                sculling,
                I arrow the deep, reach
                tip-toe for the familiar.
                Feel only a pull
                prickle my lower limbs.

I think this might be bottomless and that
I can't stand.

IN THE MOUNTAINS

I pull at you, there, dusty among books,
take and rinse you in extremes
of sun and snow, un-
clasp your tightness finger by finger
into the open palm of this pass.

Slipping city skins
we ski colours cold as ice.
Black, branch green, glacial water.
But the afternoon wears
and now it's your cupped hand,
your city weight I want
unwinding us beneath firs.

Light high up there. A verb
caught between mountains,
in place of skins we drag out.

DETAILS

Tenille, who is ten and helpful,
lifts the boxes of canning jars into the trunk
because I don't need them anymore.

It's nothing to her who has never pulled
the chain of the bare bulb onto jars astonishing
as rubies, brimming
lapis plums, white pears, cherries in juice
stickywarm and ripening

the rest of my winters. In the end
we don't decide what images follow us home.

You can see this in Marcia's work.
That opaline saltshaker bird
bought at a garage sale in the Armoury—
what is it doing in all these paintings?

REALLY ALONE

The Christmas I was nine or ten I crossed the highway
into Bowen Park and chopped down a tree. I've no idea how,
or what lark possessed me. In the end Mom gave me
an old string of lights. I wrapped gifts of ribbon candy,
arranged my dolls under icicles and angel hair,
read them Poe and the Bible. This went on for days.

Tonight in my studio, in a week late in December,
I hold a reading of works-in-progress by candlelight.
Afterwards, there's wine and cheese. I listen in the dark
to my recording. Everything goes well;
the wine a little better than the usual
reading sort, and the poet smart enough

to keep it short. Twenty-six years is a long time
between vigils; I mean being alone as a child
is alone; staging the whole thing as if an important
guest is coming. As if I could be that guest.

Which makes me think about the woman across the way
who wears aloneness in her little crocheted hat, her odd
little punches, murmurs of deference when she thinks
she's intruding. Does she conjure, like the tucked
hankie from out of her bosom, an audience? Her dead mother?
Propped dolls we shake our finger at. *Listen*, we say, *Listen here*.

WHITE BREAD AND CAKE

I'm changing my name—
try it first on the booster shot card.

Car-o-line. It sounds
Canadian. Under my pencil
the letters plump and salient
as crinolines
I long for under print
and polished cotton—not
those pleated skirts, Terlenka
plaids from Holland,
rolled at the waist for years.

Like Heather and Dawn,
Caroline has white bread
and unmottled bananas
in her lunch bag, a canopy bed,
china poodles on a white provincial dresser—O
I knew.

Mom resists my pleas,
but gives in to angel
cake from a real mix.
Teacher catches me with my finger in the icing
first greedy thing in the morning—
You can hardly be *that* hungry, dear.

continues . . .

She was right and again
when she gave my card back.
But how those starchy things
might have nourished that girl,
freed her name from its caught place
to taste rich as chocolate on the tongue.

THE NAME YOU DIDN'T WANT

One day your hair blows in your face
and the lemon smell rushes back towards
you at ten, or nine, and you chew a strand
in the old way.

And yes, your grade-school art—
the underwater world you made over and over.
A mermaid's pastel ocean, fish tinfoiled
in seaweed, shiny wrappers crumpled into
urchins and starfish. Sun-dazed
sleeper in the balm of its waves,

until *that* name, flung
like seaweed from the trolling line,
revives—
floods ugly pike and rock-cod
of the self. You know it can't fit.

But Cornelia
surprises. Undoes
the mermaid's bale into limbs
and swims till foil's shook to mirror
and there is sea.

GOLD AGAINST CARNELIAN

The air after rain no longer
scented with peony and late roses.
Summer retreats and my thoughts
clench knuckles against
you in the face of frost.

Signs. The native ash purls
red bowls into memory's green.
Tenille rakes leaves into hunches.

Just last week the jet tore a strip
across the sunfoiled sky, pitched you
up and out of my life, left
a wrinkled, hoary reflection.

I look up. So,
the colours have changed.
Snatched between gold
leaves of elm, the sky . . .
*Now I know the blue
you wanted carnelian to be.*

Tenille erupts from the leaves;
a bronze goddess scattering
medallions she squanders easily
as I would have the world
for these stones, stones.

a deep red, semi-precious stone

THE MAN I LOVE IS GOING

And in the laundromat
the women pick at trailmix,
flip glossy pages, fold towels.

And I'm glad for Saturday morning laundry,
slow heavy women who pick and flip
in the spin of tubs and drums they hear as lullabies.
Machines steamy with routine.
Slot quarters and the panel lights at whatever cycle.
You can do that here
until you feel something again.

THIRST

The earliest memory is licking
salt blocks set out in fields for cows.
Blue, indented where those long tongues rasped,
scooping saliva and salt.

I remember the tricks:
climbing with yellow boots on weathered board,
balancing on the post long enough
to locate a speck of blue
acres away. Could've been sky.

I remember sun and running and
a blade released into wind
until there was nothing
recognizable.

Except those blue blocks
I'd lie beside,
risking a salty lick.

Awful! But needed
for the long walk home,
the days of ponderous rain.

AFTER BABYSITTING, COMING HOME

She finds the key—how cold and stiff—
in its secret place and enters a room
bleached unfamiliar. Light from the street
shadows the furniture huge and distant
as grandma's old black-and-white photos.
She runs a white finger along her moon-surfaced arm;
its hairs are wild grass. And a sweet breeze
from out of the plain satisfies her approaching body,
nostrils open like an animal. As if she's been here
before, or knew she would one day. Now,
the money crisp between her panties in the drawer,
she leaves her small and sleeping parents down the hall
and follows herself
                    into long-whispered night.

2. IN THE GALLERY

(After seeing Marcia Perkins' drawings, *Studies From Life*)

1. ARTIST

And not just down into the morgue
but with optic-nerve
lent your sense for splintered bone,
havoc of flesh,
drew odd bodies, broken,
hardly breathing,
except the way this soft and freckled hand lifts
from a fleshless bone.

2. REFERENT

You are moving
pencil on paper,
lying him back to us as bones.
A pathologist decided
the particulars:

> a head (face
> averted) back
> one shoulder blade
> humerus
> elbow (with flesh)
> ulna (cleaned of flesh)
> a complete hand

Upon a table top, sometimes,
he laid that hand and touched.

3. IN THE GALLERY

"They're dead," the children say.
"The baby's dead. Yuk." A small boy
one hand clutching penis, the other
pointing chubby fingers at the glass
says: "The man cut her open and she died.
Then this one. I can tell which pictures
came first. That one (gross!)—no, this."
He skips away. The pictures will not order.

The gull at Witty's Lagoon dragged
its ripped wing, sought a harbour
not in sky, but underneath a log
away from rain and dogs. A place.
Once on that same beach, at night,
in storm and lust and soaked with spray,
hoping in our refuge flesh.
Just kids we were.

The pictures will not order.
No harbour for what's left on trolley carts.

4. KICKING STONES

Here a bare foot
anchored with a shiny bone
to pelvis (cavernous
as sea-washed burl)
waits for its shoe
and ground.

5. MAN SAWN IN 1/2

Dr. Marc says they centre the body
before the saw blade. Makes a terrible racket.
"You think cerebral lobes come ready-made?
Cross-sectioned for textbooks?" Glossed
fissures swirl like water down a drain, but
this currant nipple, still erect, this one shut eye
and splays of pubic hair clumped on either side
raise, like a blue whale out of spray, a closed hand
that points four bent fingers to the corpse's life-line,
directs the viewer to where the split head gapes.
But a thumb points obstinately past the door. It wants
out.

6. LESSON IN THE ANATOMY LAB

Cover her lower half with my hand
it's as if she's sleeping,
head tossed back over her arm.
Sleeping with the abandon of the young,
even on this trolley
with its oiled wheels.

Cover her upper half with my hand
and I see her bent legs,
brackets curved and trustfully opening
a vulva, full pink petals
jaunty with newness.

Leaning into these drawings
feels deeper than desire. O
where can I hide my nakedness?

7. WHAT WE ARE

A bunch of cavities, he says.
Aussie cheek.
Frames have always been there.
I think of conch, barnacle, mussel, clam—
all the crusted hosts of timid life.

I'm not prepared for such
flesh lying inconsequential
beneath bone cages.
These used to be people.
I touch myself, the feel is sound,
however slight this rib-flesh,
and eye my friend.

You're the dr., so tell me
this is artistic licence.
She's taking the wind out
of all the sails, pencil-keeling
us down—
right?

8. BUST

Masterpiece! Half draped,
as if the art can't contain
the black demand of line.
Such a beginning!
This one shoulder blade, stranded.
The fabric, bunched like a pillow,
or a nightie nuzzled to the neck,
ebbs from the tendril curls,
the face with the roman nose
that must have been the envy—

But she's pushed the head back
as if it's ready for resuscitation.

Sure. Mouth to mouth.

9.

Still the arm arcs
to hold that rack of ribs, split and hanging.
Things past scrutiny pulped
back onto heaps of folded skin.
Blood vessels that networked
air to lungs severed. Everything's so vacant.
Stubble in a field once aching with harvest.

The arm in death
tries to hold a man intact.

This is not altogether pathetic.

3. WHAT I KNOW OF HER

THERE ARE TIDES OF SKY THAT PULL

slim white bodies from a hat,
bare legs and arms from rubber boots,
while just-finished rain sucks
at orange-trimmed soles.

We'd been riding, had seen in the changing light
the buck moving down to the flats
to forage after sunset.
Walking back with the horses over the fields,
my girls, sturdy with chatter on either side,
clump over roots and mud. Each step's heavy
with littleness. They're so cheerful about it,
this trudging,

but I need them to want more,
to be drawn further. Or pulled,
if that's how it works. Like my mother, bent
over her garden, would look up
from weeding carrots,
or in her kitchen, pots boiling,
and with a sweep of her wrist
turn the element down, open a door
to the sky, to where the sun sets
or sky gathers and just stand there,

nothing telling her to look,
just knowing. I wonder what pact
she was making, there, over her rows.

             That vigilant watch,
this altering sky that knows the way and pulls

                    Water Valley, Alberta.

WATCHING MY MOTHER DRESS

She who loudhosannahed every chore,
cleaned and cared for us like she peeled potatoes,
in one deft spiral paring, who spun rooms
and bottles through her dusting cloth, lingered.

She herself said she had thick skin
and a broad back. But between thin straps
it was pink. I loved her then,
out of the bathroom in a gust of steam and smelling
of gingerthings that happened in the night or books.

Her back to me, that otherwise
straight-as-a-two-by-four back
looked incapable of shouldering
anything but wraps of taffeta
Jane Eyre or Austen wore.

But it could. O it could split and hoist
firewood, rake, hoe, scrub floors, keep me
pensive lest it turn in disapproval.

In her underwear she was the calla
behind french doors in the frontroom,
secret as spikes of bloom in the lily's spathe.
The silver bracelets at her wrist cold
as Rochester's touch.

She adjusted the straps.
She was a little nervous.
My mother who was never nervous, was.

SHORE-KNITTER

Footstooled at her slippered feet
like inlets beg land, I'm shown
stitches I'll need to sea-change
this ball of Adriatic blue
to some needed thing.

The sand beneath me
shifts. Uncanny
waves. The sound
her needles make, like paper clips
holding sea
to land.

HER FULL-CUPBOARD STRENGTH

Bright sails (the stiff
shiver when first you enter cold
sheets in the wind smell) that blind me
are white bolts at her shoulders; wings
clipped of want.
So white. So white.

Brave me some blue, like letters.

GRADUATION CEREMONY

Your handiwork, Grandmother.
Do you recognize
the rhinestones he bought you
that long-ago Germany weekend?
Fixing the clasp round your neck,
beads brilliant on black crêpe?

This sampler has your 1898 name.
Janna Cornelia Bol, who at nine
embroidered on red linen
all the stitches she would need.
I trace its old land ways that bent
you over your trade by ten;
threads of a knotted life. No anger
in these tiny stitches that hold
the surface.

                    My turn.
I walk on stage in a collar of light—
but within the cloth's folds my hands
grope a dark strength: fingers.

FIRST BORN

Fraser Valley, British Columbia, 1952.

She is why, we told ourselves,
we immigrate: to put plough
to imagination.
Now she's here to take it.

Somehow I don't want to give.
She doesn't see the danger—
slippery banks, how mallards
crash these sloughs and swim
beyond the farms.

Either way.
Back home her foot would stumble
on the brick of old land roads.
She wouldn't understand
the flurry in her veins
before those ruddycheeked men
of the billboards, pitchforks
in their hands, gold
shimmering behind them
far as the eye can see.

What she's seen with her blood
will surface. I give what I can:
a Canadian name.

STRAND

Hunched over hoop and embroidery linen,
she arranges seven lengths of floss on the arm rest
in descending intensity, her childish finger
hooked on new-cut teeth. She chooses blue,
brings a strand to the needle,
squints and pulls through.

I start to say—
but she shifts, or the light does,
and under the dark hair her face
is a sun-ruddied peach.

Mouth firmly closed cuts us limbs apart.
What are you thinking about?

Nothing, mother, I'm counting my stitches.

COMING FOR MOTHER

Pushing his blond hair out of his face—
Cheese Joanna. Look at Daddy—
he makes the usual adjustments.
His polaroid misses.
The lawnmower's throat's spitting green,
the tree's white petals just now.
The woman clutches her weekend
away, the seminar packet, name tag.
But when her daughter turns, runs to her—

From a second storey window I see
how tight this story is, but there are images
fixed as fragrant trees just outside the lens.
Their scent persists through all the smiles
of man and child and albumed outings.

The door on the passenger side's open.
Buckled in, the mother pulls up a knee as if climbing
sharp stairs. Her mind aches with trees too white
and in the back seat Joanna says *Mama Mama*
as if they're both learning it for the first time.

WHAT I KNOW OF HER

And what is real is humming.
You should see me step into psalms
as if I knew them.
I Will Lift Up My Eyes To The Mountains,
and I do, and they're there.
Fitting.

You saw them too
when on hands and knees
your voice into the floor
scrubbed a brilliance
we hardly dared enter.

Staccato in the clothespins,
your Dutch voice swelled
laundered sheets into billowing anthems.
So I could lie between your songs at night,
wind and sun in cotton
I still want, threadbare soft.

And I always test the new
by how the bedding
cool between my fingers
leaks *Jerusalem* . . .

4. HOW OUR FEET GO ON

1. ROTTERDAM HARBOUR, 1951

In all that crowd your handkerchief.
It fills with tears daily.
Then my grief at leaving
lurched into my hand.
Open as a wound
it groped for yours, *moeder*.

Most days I don't know
whether my face stings
with sea-spray or my own flooding.
I inhale the embroidered C
for the trace of eau de cologne
in its threads. Tenuous,
the thin lines that rail this ship,
my daughter's cot to my bunk, me to Piet.
You think you do it with your eyes open.

In my mind I've replayed our boarding
a hundred times.
Those reliable *moiliers*!
How our feet go on when the heart refuses.

2.

A thought strikes me. I'll miss your birthday.

Who'll see to the *taart* from the baker?
Who'll dress Ria? Plait her braids with red ribbon?
She won't move from her seat at the window
for fear she'll miss my bike's ring.

To think your birthday's still months away.
I'll be gone that long?

3. S.S. VOLENDAM

I should have known this was a trap.
Come with me, he said.
So why am I shut in the women's quarters
with the stench of diapers and worse?
We try to mop but when the ocean swells—
do all ships make their passengers scrub and clean?
I'm going to ask Piet the minute I see him
—and where is he? Mothers are always too late
for the deck chairs. Hennie cries and cries.
You and your *rot* idea!

4.

Tenth day at four in the afternoon—"Land!"
The deck's an instant party.
We fall over each other
hugging that first glimpse.
Piet's hat flies overboard,
headlong to shore.

5.

Snow-bound and alone in the house,
that sighting cry comes back, startles me again.
I remember the first look at the green hills
we came for. Against the November sky the relief
of those red roofs on white houses—

6.

Canada, you could use a scrub.
Sheds tacked with flattened cans
lean into grey shale.
Did they have a war here too?

From a tinny store along a cinder track,
a jar of peanut butter, bread
and oranges for the trip.

My coat sleeve smells
of this tar-and-oil-track land.
Though a salted sign
on weathered board says "Welcome."

7.

All day we press
open palms on moving pictures.
Lumber mills, towns, a car in every yard,
even an Indian, once.

The train squeezes between rocks
so big they split the sun, slide past.
And we grow prairie eyes wide as sky.

Bunked bodies tuck under overcoats
and heads prop on frumpled hats.
Even the plywood softens.

Piet leans from the upper bunk,
winks, "I'm getting closer."
I look out. "*We're* getting closer."
Fields, and ground.

8. FRASER VALLEY, B.C.

You can't imagine the shed I live in.
I'm ashamed to write.

No running water, an outhouse.
Night's the worst—the thing's
so far behind the house.
There might be bears or wolves—
who knows?

9.

Too soon for so much snow
the farmers say. But it's here—
and red shovels, chains,
a torch for thawing pipes.
Hands burn with cold.

We see the accident from behind
our steaming tea. A Chevy
(does it cross his mind to own a car
one day?) slides into the ditch.
Piet runs, sends the freezing woman in
where I, in awful English,
gesture *stove*. Her hands weep.
She gives us two dollars.

10.

Child, I watch for you,
catch your shadow
as you enter the barn to play,
mind when you come out again.
Frost over the windows.
I sit for hours breathing
a hole in ice.

11.

It's hard not to blame, but
how promising it looked on posters.

Miles of gold growing in fields
grew in us. And the stories
gossiped at the *markt*
under shade of elms and steeple.

Follow my heart's desire, you said,
but my heart stopped for the numb eternity
between "Emigrate?" and "Yes."
Now that I'm here, it's catching up.

12.

Moeder, your supplications
against cold arrived!
Knitted mitts, sweater
(its shoulder-wreath of snowflakes)
and the rooster tea-cosy.
Through your fingers,
wool gestures like a rosary.
I feel blessed.

13.

The window panes gave in
to last night's storm.

By morning our bed's
snowcovered.

14.

I should have drawn this:
a white face behind curtains
that can't close.

I couldn't have supposed
such black on white,
such a self.

I should have drawn death.

15.

Lamplight falls over Piet reading
wheat prices, politics, sports.
His absorbed figure snaps and cracks
the newsprint to attention.
He tells me things, translates black figures
until they flint the room.

I might learn to feel this as warmth,
yet more and more cold fingers
thin bones over the windows.
This season's still to be endured.
Fetch firewood, I remind him,
enough to last the night.

16.

My tears collect in puddles
on the grey linoleum, unable
to seep into earth.

On the thin walls
sepia flowers in their baskets
wither like shallow graves.

At night, above and below me,
the bedsheets crowd.
Only the merciful dark.

17.

When I wear this sweater
I think of late afternoon
in your polish-musky parlour,
dusk, the mantle clock's ticking.

Needles pulling blue
from your white fingers. You

> feel snow by the way sky gathers,
> smell it laden with itself,
> look up from knitting,
> hold out a needle, catch

the print of you I'm wearing.

18. LEIDEN

From his seat at the window
Opa will guide the neighbours
into their houses, watch them
move between rooms.

Here windows show sky and treetops.
Nothing connects to paths and roads
or women swinging their purses.

19.

A new child grows sourly in me.

Homesick every morning.
The heat of valley-summer
mirages the land into dunes
till I can't bear it.

In all these waves there must be sea.

20.

She is wrinkled as sauerkraut
in Libby jars.

All I want is your tea, mother,
in china cups with silver spoons and cream.
I don't know how to ask in English.

Sixteen hours and thirty pedalled miles later
Peter knows he has a daughter.
I drink and drink.

Give the baby your name
although she looks nothing like you.

21.

Last night I could have pitched her over the ocean.

The doctor says I've lost too much weight.
She's always at my breast.
And like this insatiable country, returns nothing.

Here, Peter. She's yours. Feed her.

22.

Mother, I've straightened
your pictures a dozen times
and again they're lopsided.
How your face leans out to me!

23.

A neighbour offers to mother
my barebones English.
I write down every new word.
Staying or not, I might as well
learn the language.

But when she kneels to wipe Hennie's face,
the child looks confused.
Only I have ever done this.

24.

Gouda on pumpernickel,
flowers from the *Veiling*, stores!
Instead, dusty shoes,
long walks nowhere.
But also chock-full ditches
the names of birds,
and a tethered goat!
Sometimes I wonder
at the sky—how did I fit
in so small a place
as Holland?

25.

I dread an empty mailbox
even more than bad news.
Is Ria ill, is your arthritis worse?
And since the news of uncle,
the *rouw kaart*, a new fear.

I need to hear, to
know *onze lieve Wilhelmina*
still lives in you.

An assured Dutch self.

26.

No frost this morning.
Another day's grace.
The first birds fly south.
I've learned to let them go,
to let new feathers soften me.

The girls growing in spite of it all.
Hennie follows her dad into the fields,
comes home with armfuls
of wheat or barley. The baby watches
me can beans and carrots.
This shoring up!

She crawls to the door,
wanting me to open it.
And then what,
I ask her brown eyes.

What I see are long roads.

GLOSSARY OF DUTCH TERMS

moeder	mother
moiliers	an imported French walking shoe fashionable in post-war Holland
taart	cake
rot	rotten
markt	open market
Opa	grandfather
Veiling	flower auction
onze lieve	our dear
rouw kaart	death announcement

5. STORY, LOVE

POEM AT CHRISTMASTIME
(the word made flesh)

I come to your room
dark as a silent piano.
Candle between us
sheds its mottled shade
on the yellow pages
of your reading
poems boundless
and therefore simple

so simple they shock,
from the foot of my childhood
bed, the voice I dreamed
and the moment I knew
if I could have anything
in the world
        (and I'd have to be rich
           for such magnificence)
I wanted each night
that male
voice out of the dark;
his stories.

I learned astonishment
with you. Once.
And therefore
forever.

MY SON

The afternoon I punish him he gathers
himself to his full five feet and stomps
between garage and car with flats of cans
I've made him sort and haul. His grim
eyes pass over me on the deck. He isn't giving
an inch; is serving life sentence in Siberia;
it's winter but he's sweating
in a thin jacket. Taking it
like a man on shoulders too slight,
hair too blond, too lovely, I think, to ride safely
cross town to the Stampede grounds.
He concentrates on the tray stacked
tremulously high with jittery cans
as if it were a trick with blades he can
finally show me. His back
stiffens with disdain for the enemy
and I realize I am the enemy, cast
among those who would harm him.
He leans into the gate to push it open
with shoulders

        that one day must square up
at the door of the room where somebody
lays dying, or is leaving, or begs him ask
the saving question.

Under his sudden power hinges
swing, gate gives, and he is thrust
forward. I hold my breath for the crash,
but there is none, for now. Quick,
young legs have steadied him against
that wobbling world he joined
when first he shrugged—so casually—his shoulders.

LETTING BETSY GO

A trade-in.
After the test drive worth only a hundred
instead of three.

Scraping frost from the glass
on those first drives. Just enough
to see what I needed.

Fingers wedged in the window slot,
I pulled hard with just my tips
to close the door.

You'll have to sit beside me, the seatbelt's broken.
My professor slides over like a round, sweet date,
says: *Don't try anything!* I squeeze his knee.

This rust-coloured Buick in the driveway
my only constant while houses
heart and cities changed.

Full moon through the window.
Diet of Strange Places on the radio.
Long kissing on a low and bending bench.

I brake for one, two, three hares across the road,
white and bounding out of Grimm.
I should have expected this. You are with me.

Service attendants are like short movies.
Their serious faces small boats, awash.
Oar-arms dip, dip

into the belted past of miles of needing something.
Gone. The new car's more efficient,
uses less of everything.

CHOIR ROBES

Sunday, and the choristers' gowns
hung on pegs, their white bibs breaches of gloom.
The number board with last week's hymns
was propped against a bolt of cloth
I couldn't tell was anything but folds.
I didn't go in, though I'm drawn
to light that through
the lintel merges
into a kind of
stained glass
story.

        And there were flowers,
tiny, white, a common shrub growing outside
the arched door held open by a stone.

PHOTOGRAPH OF A SPLIT-FERN

Plans chipped as the old ache
in your back, you look past
the stuffed-heart comfort
home is. Out beyond
the drapes to Three Sisters
splitting sky.

You want it all: the Sunday drive
with the family, the mountains
your eyes' pleasure take.

They wouldn't come, couldn't go.
The kids are getting older, your wife said.
Doesn't matter, you said, sulky, staring.
The cinnamon bun untouched,
coffee filming as it cools.

What caught you—a last stab,
its slant on a leaf or two
of this green crabby thing?
Greedy for light,
for what's left
of day.

NEW WORLD

She's determined to love even the inherited brow;
sealed wings across the eyes. Her own she plucks
to ease the heaviness. She needn't have worried.
Her baby's beautiful, narrow and dark,
as if native to this land.

And again and again she's surprised by this
daughter who carries herself as if she belongs
to long and coltish legs or straightbacked to the piano.
Under her fingers the black keys are the sound of wings.

But today the girl brings David home—
dull-eyed, feet turned inward—
and again the mother sees pell-melling behind her
all those brighthaired boys.
What makes us choose

against ourselves? But already
birds beat upward, inhabit her. And this child
with thick dark hair banged on a square descending face.

UNLOVELY BEHIND THE DOOR

Two years later she'll learn
from the chaplain's daughter the word
for what the neighbour's teenage son
big as her father did to her.

But right now she's in bed with her clothes on,
a yellow sweater with eighteen buttons
in need of doing up and pedalpushers.
Till Dad gets home.

Hears the scrape of knives
on dinner plates,
the cabbage smells.
Her belly aches.
Hears the newspaper
crackle in his hand,
her sister's goodnight, and now
he'll come for sure.
She'll say sorry all right.
Her mother's tight lips
that afternoon make her
wrap armsround,
draw up her knees.
He'll come.
His storm will out
the bad. For sure.

continues . . .

But she hears bed-springs,
voices leaving her
alone with what was done.
Father. Father.
She'd tear her insides out
to bring him.

When finally morning comes
those whittled legs,
thin arms and hands,
open the door. Turning there,

her up-and-down finger
bids propped dolls wait
till she comes for them after school.

THE TIME I KNEW YOU LONG BEFORE WE MET

You drove along the Gorge
the night of Elvis' death,
tourist in your rented car
not knowing me; I at the Sherwood,
eating some farewell meal
for an office mate I've long forgotten,
not knowing you.

Were you that man in the lobby
coming unreasonably close, a stranger
I must not touch

my arms already full
of coffee trays, the office girls, O you know
the safe and recognizable?

Like our meeting now,
some things start a sudden ache.
You trouble me. Still.

A SONG THAT'S OVER TOO SOON

Tonight you travel to another country.
The tape you pulled
to play this afternoon, then didn't,
is now half done playing your song.
I see a face in a fast cab
and on the floor the map's dark veins
spreading between us in so many directions
are bleary; wet ink on watercolour.

All routes evaporate? Impossible
as your scent disappearing
from your robe, this room,
into a suitcase, a plane.

While I listen your finger
loses the red-felt trail,
presses a spot
not on any map.

DOUBLES

He loved sweat.
Would swipe a trickle,
fingertrace its course,
lick the salty tendons
of a neck strained
in serve. Kiss a springing
circle at the throat—
that rash of beads.
Bursting.

He claimed the language
of sweat (breathless
under talc, odorous cologne).
That which is clean.
The sweat of children,
damp nighties, clutched fingers.
What we are
clothes off and dancing.

THE BRIDGE YOU FORGOT

These are the instruments
you forbid me to touch:
slide rule, level, triangle. They lie
beside blueprints in your desk.

Against your wooden
edge, pencil lines thinner
than any school-ruler spell
my world. One step
and over the falls
that drag at me
their undertow.

Niagara
in the clear alcohol of the level
moves slowly from one wooden side to another;
a ship crossing the ocean all afternoon.

You build bridges. *Second Narrows, Dominion,*
and the one through the Pass.
Your father-hand spanning the steel

made safe crossing
for all the people in cars,
but my rigged passage:
a locked drawer, a fisted key.

AFTER MESSIAH

Nothing but our own
heaviness
silences like this.
Numbed in applause,
the last *Amen* translates
to shuffles
in the aisle, arms
struggling with wraps.

Hand brushes
a knee, but the gesture's
past heeding. How resolutions
blur as frost forests
the windshield. Too weary
to scrape, we watch
breath run down in rivulets
on weeping glass.

LOVE LETTERS
       (her first, my last)

At the end of the day
it's too late for anything,
Danielle in bed and half asleep
uncurls her fingers. Read this, Mom.

                    Hello my dear. How are you? Dumb question.
                    I just saw you two hours ago.

I sit beside her.
The fixture on the nighttable
shaped like a traffic light yellows
the posters, the jewel box; flashes
green over dolls' porcelain faces
and this narrow bed.

Your letter came. I read it.
When I looked up I saw
winterlight strike its metal breakers
through the leaves and I knew
summer was over.

Everything's been said then?
Overhead, those clouds.
That heavy silent time before rain . . .
only this time there'll be no rain.
Or words. All those unused words;
grey blisters on my tongue
and skin; that red and glowing
shutter of the self.

I fold both letters.
Ben's, throbbing in the red light
of the little signal lamp, I offer
into her cupped palm.
Closing round it like a conch
her fingers hold the ocean.
Her fisted hand the size of a heart;
a lit desire; now red now green.

I'LL NEVER LIVE WHERE IT DOESN'T SNOW

Remember when my house was garden
full: mums purple as these,
bouquets of gold seed and stem,
roses once in the hey-day?

But this is another country
where frost's archangel
mouth over shaggy-headed marigolds
spits burnt-match stems.

I've clawed and crawled
back for a garden echo. I know now
I must go

with stubble. To a further
window, where a cactus
pushes tuber-celled
from sand.

POSTCARD FROM THE READING ROOM, BRITISH LIBRARY

Under the fifth skylight window to the right
of the clock where I work . . . I imagine
your winter scarf (the smell of wool
on my neck, Edworthy's grove, walks
by the Bow) over the chairback.
Pen in hand, your arm moves,
cuts phrases, a shape or conjunction.
The disjunction is you in that country.

Just a postcard, paper thin.
I hold it to the light and for a moment . . .
No. There's all the world between
the scratch of wool and the way
your pen has formed this C,
spread thinly over so much.

"IF YOU EVER GET TO TBILSK I WILL SHOW YOU WHAT I MEAN"

Your letter
like a peacock's fan unfolds
the feeling of what might be.
Out of the piano hall
where we stood back to back,
light moves its white-note-flurry,
draws each cell of my body.
Ahead, the grey Atlantic.

Paper boats
from half way round the world
sail me further than I've ever been.
What stand out most clearly
are stones. Grey and individual
they rise mountainous. Out of
place and balance.

And now this outpost. Ironic,
surely, that however long-way-round,
our bodies, like insects to bright flowering,
pull till we are face to face.
I will go as far as Tbilsk.
Expect me.